SCOTTIE BOOKS

MARY, QUEEN OF SCOTS

ACTIVITY BOOK

By Elizabeth Douglas
Illustrated by Carrie Philip

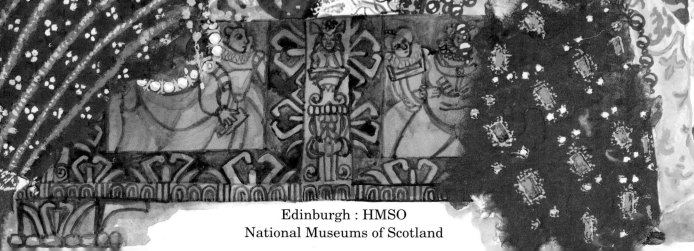

Edinburgh : HMSO
National Museums of Scotland

Mary, Queen of Scots – Family Tree

The links between the throne of Scotland and the throne of England were close. Mary, Queen of Scots' grandmother was the sister of King Henry VIII of England.

King James V became ruler of Scotland when he was just two years old. It is said that James V liked to dress up as a peasant and go out into the countryside. He did this so that he could hear what his people were saying about him.

Mary of Guise was James V's second wife. She came from a very important French family. James V and Mary of Guise had two sons, James and Robert, who both died before their daughter, Mary, was born.

James IV of

Mary of Guise = James V of

Henry, Lord Darnley = Mary, Queen of Scots = Francis II of

?

Why not try working out your own family tree?

A person whose job is to discover people's family tree is called a genealogist

2

Henry VIII was the King of England at the time of Mary's birth. King Henry VIII of England was Mary's great-uncle.

King Henry VIII of England wanted to rule Scotland as well as England. He thought that if his son, Edward, married Mary, Queen of Scots, this would give him power over Scotland.

Some people thought that Mary, Queen of Scots should be Queen of England as well. In later years this claim was to cause problems between Queen Mary and Queen Elizabeth I of England.

Long live King James

I agree

me too

GENEALOGIST? How many words can you make using the letters in

3

The Birth of Mary, Queen of Scots – Linlithgow Palace

Mary was born on 8th December 1542 in Linlithgow Palace. Six days later she became Mary, Queen of Scots. Her father, King James V of Scotland, died on 14th December. Three weeks earlier he had been beaten by an English army at the Battle of Solway Moss.

Mary was far too young to rule Scotland herself. She was only a baby. A noble was given the job of ruling Scotland until Mary was old enough to rule. This noble was called a Regent. Mary's mother wanted to be Regent but the job was given to the Earl of Arran. He was a relative of Mary. At the time of Mary's birth Arran was heir to the throne of Scotland.

This is a picture of what Linlithgow Palace might have looked like at the time of Mary's birth.

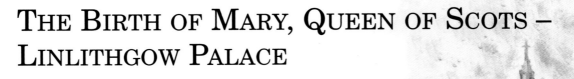

Can you find eight pond creatures hiding in the picture of Linlithgow Palace? (Answers on page 40.)

You can see these coats of arms above the gateway leading from the town to the Palace.

THE CORONATION OF QUEEN MARY

In the days when Mary, Queen of Scots was a baby, it was not unusual for children to get married. If two different countries wanted to become friendlier, a prince and princess from the two countries might get married.

King Henry VIII of England wanted his son Edward, who was five years old, to marry Queen Mary, who was only a few months old. The Scots and the English agreed that when Queen Mary was 10, she would go to England. Many people thought that Henry VIII might try to kidnap Mary before the 10 years had gone by. Mary of Guise wanted to take her baby daughter to a safe place so that she would come to no harm.

In August 1543 Mary's mother decided to take her to Stirling Castle. It was a safe place, sitting on a high rock like Edinburgh Castle. One month later Mary was crowned Queen of Scotland, in the Chapel Royal in Stirling Castle. She was just nine months old.

At the coronation of Queen Mary, the Earl of Arran carried the crown, the Earl of Lennox carried the sceptre and the Earl of Argyll carried the sword of state. Cardinal Beaton crowned Queen Mary.

Earl of Argyll

The Scottish Crown Jewels contain many precious gems. Do you know the colours of these precious stones? Diamond Amethyst Ruby Emerald Peridot Sapphire Garnet

Cardinal Beaton

nnoX

7

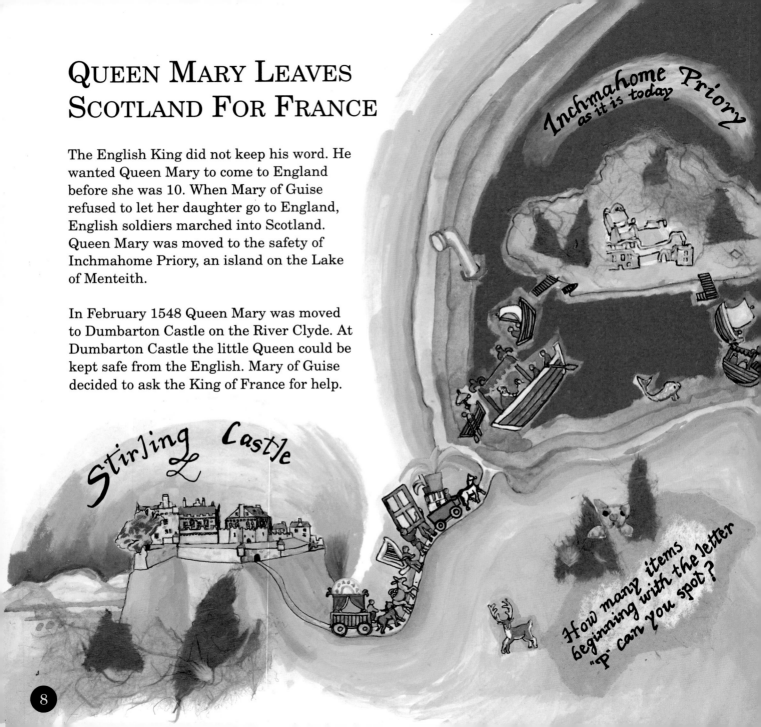

QUEEN MARY LEAVES SCOTLAND FOR FRANCE

The English King did not keep his word. He wanted Queen Mary to come to England before she was 10. When Mary of Guise refused to let her daughter go to England, English soldiers marched into Scotland. Queen Mary was moved to the safety of Inchmahome Priory, an island on the Lake of Menteith.

In February 1548 Queen Mary was moved to Dumbarton Castle on the River Clyde. At Dumbarton Castle the little Queen could be kept safe from the English. Mary of Guise decided to ask the King of France for help.

Inchmahome Priory
as it is today

Stirling Castle

How many items beginning with the letter "p" can you spot?

King Henry II of France said he would help Scotland if his four-year-old son, Francis, married Queen Mary, who was then six years old.

The French King sent his own royal ship along with 100 other ships to take Queen Mary to France. The French ships took a route which avoided places where they might meet English ships. On 7th August 1548 Queen Mary sailed from Dumbarton, leaving Scotland for the first time. Mary of Guise did not go to France with her daughter. She stayed in Scotland to help govern the country while her daughter, Queen Mary, was away.

Queen Mary was not going to France alone. Along with all the adults, who would look after the Queen, there were four little girls. These four girls were to become close friends of the Queen. They were called Mary Seton, Mary Beaton, Mary Livingstone and Mary Fleming.

Can you find the right way from the pier to the flag at the top of Dumbarton Rock?

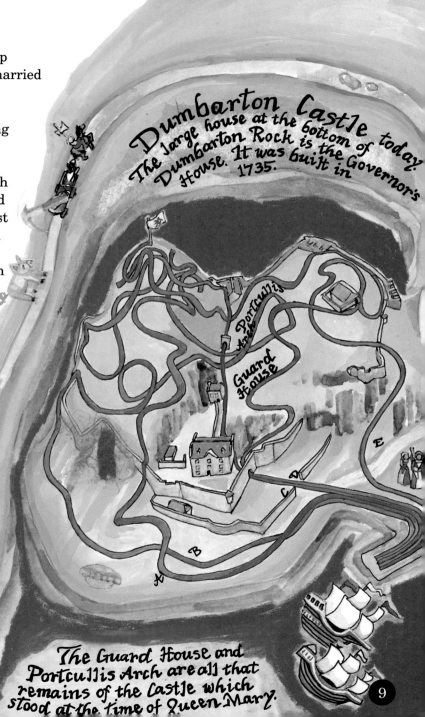

Dumbarton Castle today. The large house at the bottom of Dumbarton Rock is the Governor's House. It was built in 1735.

The Guard House and Portcullis Arch are all that remains of the castle which stood at the time of Queen Mary.

QUEEN MARY'S LIFE IN FRANCE

Queen Mary arrived in France on 13th August 1548. She travelled through the north of France to a castle where the French royal children were staying. The castle was at Carrières near Saint-Germain. It was there that Queen Mary met her future husband, the Dauphin Francis, for the first time. Dauphin was the title given to the heir to the throne of France. Francis was a small, pale boy of four. Queen Mary liked Francis from the start and treated him like her little brother.

Queen Mary and the Dauphin got officially engaged on 11th April 1558. Their wedding took place two weeks later at Notre-Dame Cathedral, Paris. Queen Mary was 15 and the Dauphin was 14. Queen Mary wore a beautiful white dress and lots of sparkling jewellery. After the marriage she became known as Queen Dauphiness.

For a year Queen Mary led a happy life as Queen Dauphiness but it was soon to change. Three tragedies touched her life one after the other.

The French royal children had many pets. There were always lots of little dogs scurrying around. How many small dogs can you see in the picture? (Answer on page 40.)

King Henry II of France died in June 1559. He had been taking part in a jousting tournament and had been fatally wounded. Queen Mary thus became Queen of France as well as Queen of Scotland. On 11th June 1560 Queen Mary's mother, Mary of Guise, died in Edinburgh. Lastly, her husband, Francis, died on 5th December 1560. He had come home from a day's hunting with an earache. This turned into a more serious illness from which he did not recover.

Queen Mary had a difficult decision to make. Should she stay in France or should she return to the country of her birth? She was visited in France by her half-brother, Lord James Stewart. He brought with him an invitation for her to return to Scotland, from the Lords who were governing the country. Queen Mary decided to return to Scotland and govern the country herself.

QUEEN MARY RETURNS TO SCOTLAND

On a misty August morning in 1561 two French galleys sailed into Leith harbour. On one of the ships was Mary, Queen of Scots. It was 13 years since Queen Mary had been in Scotland.

There was nobody waiting to meet Queen Mary. The ships had arrived earlier than expected. The Queen was shown into the house of a rich merchant called Andrew Lamb. A messenger was sent to Lord James, the Queen's half-brother, to tell him that she had arrived.

The Queen travelled through the streets of Edinburgh to Holyrood Palace. The people of Edinburgh cheered when they saw their Queen. She was a tall, beautiful woman dressed in black.

What message did the French galleys have for the Scottish people? Use the flag alphabet to find out.

12

Queen Mary and her followers returned to Scotland in 2 large galleys. One was painted white the other red.

Queen Mary and Her Four Maries

The first evening that Queen Mary was back in Scotland, a crowd of Edinburgh people sang songs and played music for her outside the gates of Holyrood Palace. They came back for a few nights after that, too. The people were very pleased that their Queen had come home.

The 'Four Maries', Mary Seton, Mary Beaton, Mary Livingstone and Mary Fleming, returned from France with Queen Mary. They became the Queen's ladies-in-waiting at Holyrood Palace.

Queen Mary had many ways of keeping herself amused in the evenings in Holyrood Palace. She enjoyed playing billiards, backgammon, chess and cards. Queen Mary also liked to dress up or disguise herself. Once the Queen and the 'Four Maries' dressed up as merchants' wives and went out into the streets of Edinburgh. Queen Mary also put on plays with her own set of puppets.

Queen Mary and her 'Four Maries' often spent the evenings playing games like backgammon or working on their embroidery.

There is a well-known nursery rhyme which was supposedly written abo[ut] Queen Mary and her 'Four Mar[ies]. Do you know what it is? (Answer on page 40.)

Holyrood Palace today

14

silver bells

cockle shells

Queen Mary's Bath House. It is beside the main road at the edge of the Palace grounds at Holyrood.

Queen Mary's Bath House

15

Queen Mary and John Knox

When Queen Mary returned to Scotland in August 1561 most people were overjoyed to see her. There was one man who did not share their joy. He was John Knox, the Protestant preacher. John Knox was a leading member of the Protestant Church.

While Queen Mary was in France there had been great religious changes in Scotland. Many people had been unhappy with the Roman Catholic Church. Among these people were a group of leading Scottish noblemen, including Queen Mary's half-brother, Lord James Stewart, and John Knox. John Knox joined the Protestant Church which grew very popular in the years that Queen Mary was away. On August 17th 1560 the Protestant Church became the official Church in Scotland. Roman Catholics who stayed faithful to their Church had to worship in private as the public saying of Mass had been banned. Queen Mary was a devout Roman Catholic. John Knox was not happy to see her because he did not want Scotland to return to the Catholic Church.

As the Queen's chief adviser at the time, Lord James Stewart was present at the first meeting between Queen Mary and John Knox.

John Knox

Queen Mary tried to deal with the question of religion soon after her return. She said she would like things to stay as they were in Scotland, but that she would like to worship as she pleased in private. This did not satisfy John Knox. He preached a sermon which made very clear what he thought of the Catholic Church. This led to his first stormy meeting with the Queen. They met four more times. These meetings usually took place after John Knox had preached a sermon that Queen Mary disagreed with.

Did you know?

John Knox was born in Haddington in about 1514. He studied at St Andrews University. One surprising fact about John Knox is that he was a galley slave for almost two years. He was taken prisoner in 1547 after the siege of St Andrews Castle had ended. It is also thought that he knew about the plan to murder David Riccio.

John Knox House
Edinburgh.

17

Queen Mary's Travels

In August 1562 Queen Mary decided that she would like to make a progress, or royal tour, of the north of Scotland. On 12th August 1562 the Queen set out from Holyrood Palace. A few of the places she visited before reaching Aberdeen were Linlithgow, Stirling, Perth and Glamis.

The Queen had another reason for visiting the north of Scotland. One of the noble families of that area was causing trouble. The Earl of Huntly, who was a Catholic, thought that the Queen was being too nice to the Protestants in Scotland and said so publicly. He was, also, not pleased that the Queen had given the title of the Earl of Moray to her half-brother, Lord James Stewart. The new Earl of Moray's land bordered on to Huntly's land. Huntly had been making a lot of money from this land in the past, and now it was the Earl of Moray's. Also Huntly's son, John Gordon, had committed a crime in Edinburgh and had escaped from prison. The Queen was not very pleased with the Earl of Huntly or his son.

After visiting Inverness the Queen returned to Aberdeen, closely followed by John Gordon. John Gordon planned to kidnap the Queen and marry her. At Aberdeen the Queen received some worrying news – the Earl of Huntly was gathering an army. He planned to march to Aberdeen, kidnap the Queen and marry

her to whomever he wanted. The Queen was furious. She sent for her own troops so that she could deal with the Earl of Huntly and his son.

On 28th October 1562 at Corrichie, near Aberdeen, the Earl of Moray and the Earl of Maitland led the Queen's army into battle. The battle was won quickly by the Queen's army. Huntly and his son were taken prisoner, and soon after the Earl of Huntly collapsed and died. His son, John Gordon, was put on trial in Edinburgh. He was found guilty of treason and executed.

In the picture you can see Queen Mary returning home after a day spent hunting in the Forest of Falkland. You may have noticed that there are a few things wrong with the picture. There are things in the picture which belong to our time, not Queen Mary's. There are nine 'wrong things'. Can you find them? (Answers on page 40.)

Falkland Palace today

The Queen's Room

Real Tennis Court

During her reign Queen Mary visited many places in Scotland. One of the places she visited most often was Falkland Palace. The Queen liked to go hunting in the Forest of Falkland.

Mary's first husband dies

Mary returns to Scotland

The French King dies

Go back 1

Mary argues with John Knox

Mary is sent to France - she marries the Dauphin

Mary is crowned Queen of Scotland

Miss a turn

Move forward

Miss a turn

English armies march into Scotland

Race for the Throne

Mary marries Lord Darnley

King James V of Scotland dies

Go back 1

Rules: For this game you will need – a coin and counters. To move – toss the coin – heads move 2 spaces/tails move 1 space. This game is played in the same way as "Snakes and Ladders". The winner is the player who reaches the throne first.

LORD DARNLEY

On her return to Scotland in 1561, Queen Mary knew that she had a difficult job ahead. After a year of ruling the country on her own she decided it was time that she got married again. Queen Mary needed someone to help her govern Scotland.

Queen Mary's first choice for a new husband was Don Carlos, heir to the Spanish throne. This would have given Scotland a powerful ally. This choice, however, did not please Queen Elizabeth of England. Queen Elizabeth had her own suggestion to make. She hinted that if Queen Mary accepted Queen Elizabeth's choice of husband she would think about making Mary her heir. This was something that Queen Mary wanted above all else. Queen Elizabeth suggested Robert Dudley, Earl of Leicester, as a suitable marriage partner. However, in February 1565 Queen Mary met another young man. His name was Henry Stewart, Lord Darnley.

Lord Darnley was a cousin of Queen Mary. His father was the Earl of Lennox and his mother was Lady Margaret Douglas. Queen Mary and Lord Darnley shared the same grandmother, Margaret Tudor, sister of King Henry VIII of England. Lord Darnley was a tall, fair-haired young man with fine courtly manners.

Queen Mary was served with four helpings of each dish. She would eat one helping and the rest would be given to the poor.

Queen Mary still had not made a decision about who should be her new husband. Don Carlos could no longer be chosen because he was very ill. Queen Mary was disappointed about this news, but not as disappointed as she was going to become. A message arrived from the English Queen which said that even if Queen Mary did marry the Earl of Leicester she would not become heir to the English throne. Queen Mary was very, very angry at this news. She turned all her attention to Lord Darnley.

As time went by, it became clear that Lord Darnley was not such a nice person as he had first appeared. He was proud and moody. Many people tried to persuade Queen Mary not to marry him but she had made up her mind.

Queen Mary and Lord Darnley were married on 29th July 1565 at Holyrood Palace. The service was held at six o'clock in the morning. Darnley left the chapel after the main service was over. He was a Protestant, and so did not stay to hear Mass with the Queen. In the afternoon a big wedding reception was held for Queen Mary and her new husband in the Palace.

Here is a list of ingredients which Queen Mary's cooks might have used. Do you know which are food and which are used to flavour food?

nutmeg oysters olive oil pike
vinegar eel
broth perch cloves
snails marjoram capon
pigeon salmon broth toadfish mutton saffron
porpoise catfish
goose partridge

The Murder of David Riccio

Perhaps Queen Mary should have listened to her friends when they advised her not to marry Lord Darnley. Her life became more difficult from the day she married him. The Queen's half-brother, the Earl of Moray, and Darnley did not like each other. The problems between them got so bad that Moray and some of his friends had to leave Scotland.

Queen Mary decided that the Earl of Moray and his friends should have their lands taken from them for the trouble they had caused. The Lords, loyal to Moray, did not like this at all. They decided to take matters into their own hands. The Lords thought up a plan to involve Darnley in the murder of the Queen's secretary, David Riccio. First of all they encouraged Darnley to believe he was being unfairly treated by the Queen. Darnley wanted more power than Queen Mary was prepared to give him. Then they started a rumour that Queen Mary was getting far too friendly with David Riccio. The plan worked and Darnley was so annoyed with his wife that he agreed to take part in the murder of her secretary. David Riccio was Italian. He had come to Queen Mary's court in 1561. Riccio was

an ambitious man and worked his way up through the Queen's household. Riccio became Queen Mary's private secretary in 1564. The Lords, who were unhappy about what had happened to the Earl of Moray, did not like Riccio. They thought he had too much power for someone from his background.

By the beginning of March 1566 Queen Mary was living very quietly at Holyrood. She was expecting a baby in June of that year and could not go out as often as before. On the evening of 9th March Queen Mary and her friends were sitting in the Queen's private rooms in Holyrood Palace. David Riccio was with them. They were just about to eat when a noise disturbed them. It came from the stairs which led from the Queen's rooms. The curtain moved and Darnley came into the room. Soon after he was followed by other men. Darnley held the Queen aside while the other men murdered David Riccio. He was stabbed 56 times. Queen Mary was extremely upset and angry. The next day Darnley came to her to say he was very sorry for what had happened. He also told her that, following David Riccio's murder, the Lords planned to take her to Stirling Castle and hold her there until her baby was born. The Queen forgave Darnley for his part in the murder and decided to leave Holyrood Palace for both her own and for her baby's safety.

If you go on a tour of Holyrood Palace look out for a small doorway and stairs which Darnley and the other murderers used on the night of David Riccio's murder. It is next to the doorway which you use to go into the Queen's bed chamber.

THE BIRTH OF PRINCE JAMES

With the help of a group of loyal friends, Queen Mary and Darnley escaped from Holyrood Palace, a few days after Riccio's murder. They left in the middle of the night and headed for Dunbar Castle. Queen Mary and her husband returned to Edinburgh on 18th March leading a large army. By the time they reached the city David Riccio's murderers had already fled.

Queen Mary no longer felt safe in Holyrood Palace so she moved into Edinburgh Castle. It was there on 19th June 1566 that the Queen gave birth to a baby boy. He was called James, named after the Queen's father. The whole of Scotland rejoiced. Now there was an heir to the throne of Scotland.

Cameo pendant of Mary Queen of Scots

Traquair House

Traquair House

Cradle used by Queen Mary for her son, James.

Queen Mary's Ho Jedburgh.

26

Later on in the summer of that year, Queen Mary went stag hunting at Traquair along with a group of noblemen. John Stewart, the Laird of Traquair, was the captain of the Queen's guard at Holyrood Palace, and he had helped the Queen escape after Riccio's murder. The Queen and her husband were not getting on very well. Darnley did not join the Queen stag hunting until later in the summer. When he did arrive he argued with the Queen and was unkind to her.

In October 1566 Queen Mary went on a royal tour of the Scottish border towns. While visiting Jedburgh the Queen became very ill. The people with her thought that she might die. It was only the quick thinking of the Queen's French doctor that saved her life and helped her to get well.

If you get a chance to go to either Traquair House or Mary, Queen of Scots' House in Jedburgh, see if you can find these items reputedly connected with Queen Mary.

Edinburgh Castle

Rosary and crucifix belonging to Queen Mary, Traquair House.

Queen Mary's Death Mask, Mary Queen of Scots' House, Jedburgh.

Kirk o' Field

When Queen Mary returned to Edinburgh she decided to stay at Craigmillar Castle, on the outskirts of the city. There she had a meeting with a group of the most important Scottish Lords. They talked about Darnley and the way he was behaving. He was not behaving in the way a King of Scotland should. At the christening of Prince James, Darnley behaved particularly badly. The christening took place on 17th December 1566 in the Chapel Royal in Stirling Castle. Darnley did not agree with Queen Mary's choice of godparents for his son, so he refused to go to the christening. He left Stirling for Glasgow, where he became seriously ill.

Queen Mary decided that she would try to sort out the problems between herself and Darnley. When Darnley returned to Edinburgh on 1st February 1567 he stayed in a house at Kirk o' Field, just inside the city walls. Darnley was to stay at Kirk o' Field until he was completely well. On Sunday 9th February Queen Mary came to see if Darnley was well enough to return to Holyrood Palace.

That day the Queen was very busy. One of her servants was getting married and she had an important dinner to go to in the afternoon. In the evening the Queen went to visit Darnley at Kirk o' Field. The Queen would have liked to stay longer with her husband but she was

Lord Darnley

Can you solve this puzzle? What does the message say?

(Answer on page 40.)

reminded that she had to return to the Palace. The Queen was going to the evening entertainment at her servant's wedding.

Around two o'clock in the morning Edinburgh was shaken by a loud explosion. The explosion came from the direction of Kirk o' Field. The first people to get there saw that the house in which Darnley had been staying had been blown up. The house had been destroyed. People searched among the ruins but no sign of Darnley could be found. Eventually, the bodies of Darnley and his servant were found in the garden at the back of the house. It looked as if they had been trying to escape. There were no marks on their bodies to show that they had been in an explosion. They had been strangled.

Did you know?
The houses at Kirk o' Field stood where the Edinburgh University buildings stand today at the corner of Chambers Street and the South Bridge in Edinburgh city centre.

The bodies of Darnley and his servant were found in the garden at the back of the house.

THE EARL OF BOTHWELL AND CARBERRY HILL

There was one Scottish nobleman who was always at Queen Mary's side at this troubled time. He was James Hepburn, Earl of Bothwell. The Queen valued his help, but many people did not trust him. They thought he was to blame for the explosion at Kirk o' Field. The Queen was warned, by her friends, of what people might think if she became too friendly with Bothwell. Posters began to go up around Edinburgh linking the Queen and Bothwell with Darnley's murder. Bothwell turned out to have plans of his own. He wanted to marry Queen Mary.

On 20th April 1567 Queen Mary and her courtiers travelled to Stirling Castle to visit the baby Prince James. Stirling Castle served as the nursery for many Scottish royal children. Prince James was to spend most of his childhood there. The Queen's return journey was brought to a halt by a band of men led by Bothwell. He kidnapped the Queen and took her and a few of her courtiers to Dunbar Castle.

Queen Mary and the Earl of Bothwell returned to Edinburgh on 6th May 1567. On 15th May they were married in Holyrood Palace. Just over three months had passed since the death of Darnley, the Queen's second husband.

There are two men on the right of the picture who look almost the same. Spot five differences between them.

The other Scottish Lords thought that Bothwell was not a suitable husband for Queen Mary. They also did not like the fact that he had kidnapped her. The Lords decided it would be best if Bothwell was punished. They took their soldiers and marched to Borthwick Castle where Queen Mary and her new husband were staying. The castle was surrounded by the Lords' army. Queen Mary and Bothwell made a plan. While the Queen spoke to the Lords, Bothwell escaped. In the middle of the night Queen Mary escaped from the castle dressed as a man. Bothwell and Queen Mary met up again at Dunbar Castle.

The Queen realised that she was in danger of losing her throne so she began to gather her own army. At Carberry, just outside Musselburgh, on 15th June 1567, the Queen's army met the Lords' army. The Lords demanded that if the Queen wanted things to go back to normal she would have to leave Bothwell. Faced with this choice the Queen persuaded Bothwell to flee.

Queen Mary returned to Edinburgh with the Lords. She was greeted with shouts and jeers from people as she entered the city. Queen Mary realised that she was the Lords' prisoner – instead of being taken to Holyrood Palace she was shut in a small room of the Provost's house.

LOCHLEVEN CASTLE

Queen Mary was the prisoner of the Lords. They had tricked her into leaving Bothwell in exchange for her freedom. From the Provost of Edinburgh's house she was taken briefly to Holyrood Palace and then on to the island castle of Lochleven, in Fife. Lochleven Castle was the home of the Douglas family.

Queen Mary was very ill during the first few weeks on the island. People thought that she might die. It was during the Queen's illness that she was forced to sign abdication papers. This meant that Queen Mary had given up her throne. On 29th July 1567 Prince James was crowned King of Scotland. King James VI was just over one year old. The Queen's half-brother, the Earl of Moray, became Regent.

Queen Mary never gave up hope that one day she might be free again. It seems that there were people in the castle willing to help her. Two friends that the Queen made in the castle were George and Willie Douglas. George was the brother of the Laird of Lochleven. Willie Douglas was a poor relative of the family who worked as the Laird's personal servant.

Queen Mary first tried to escape from Lochleven Castle towards the end of March 1568. She left the island disguised as a washer woman. It was the Queen's fine hands that gave her away.

Queen Mary left the castle by the postern gate. She was in disguise.

Willie Douglas led everyone in a game of "The Lord of Misrule". This game was like "Follow my Leader." Willie did not want anyone to see the horsemen gathering on the shore.

Willie Douglas stole the keys to the castle. The castle gates were locked at seven o'clock every evening. No guards were on duty after that time.

George and Willie Douglas' escape plan was very clever. If you had been a prisoner in the castle how would you have escaped?

32

Willie rowed the boat across the Loch. George Douglas was waiting on the shore with a horse for the Queen.

The boatman took the Queen back to the island but did not tell anyone what had happened. Queen Mary's second attempt was successful. She escaped from Lochleven Castle on 2nd May 1568, with the help of George and Willie Douglas.

THE BATTLE OF LANGSIDE

Queen Mary wanted her throne back. The Scottish nobles who had helped the Queen escape from Lochleven Castle were joined by others. At the head of a large army, Queen Mary marched to Glasgow, where the Regent Moray was staying. She would have to defeat him if she wanted her throne back.

The Regent came to meet the Queen with his own army. His army was smaller than Queen Mary's but it was more organised. The two armies met at a village called Langside, just south of Glasgow, on 13th May 1568. As the battle was about to begin, one of Queen Mary's generals fainted. His men fled. There was confusion in the rest of the army. The Queen went among the men to encourage them but they were arguing with each other. The Queen could see she had lost the battle and fled.

Queen Mary headed for south-west Scotland. The people in that part of the country were still loyal to her. With the help of her followers, Queen Mary left Scotland, on 16th May 1568, for the second and last time. She was 26 years old. Mary decided to ask Queen Elizabeth for help. The English Queen had sent friendly messages during Queen Mary's imprisonment in Lochleven Castle. At this point Queen Mary was still hopeful that her fortunes would change. Little did she know that she was to spend the rest of her life as a prisoner.

Here are 6 anagrams. They are mixed-up names of places in Scotland connected with Queen Mary. Can you work them out?

1. IOILLYHWGN
2. GLINRIST
3. BINERDUGH
4. KDLFALNA
5. EELVOCNLH
6. BNADMORUL

Answers on page 40

Batt of Langi

Queen Mary spent her last night in Scotland at Dundren Abbey

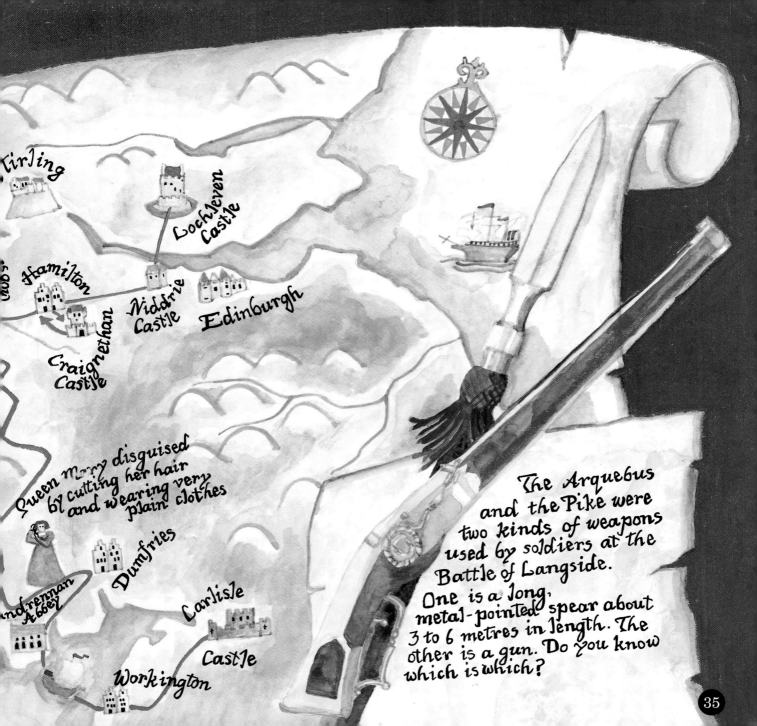

Stirling

Lochleven Castle

Hamilton

Niddrie Castle

Edinburgh

Craignethan Castle

Queen Mary disguised by cutting her hair and wearing very plain clothes

Dumfries

Dundrennan Abbey

Carlisle

Carlisle Castle

Workington

The Arquebus and the Pike were two kinds of weapons used by soldiers at the Battle of Langside.

One is a long, metal-pointed spear about 3 to 6 metres in length. The other is a gun. Do you know which is which?

ENGLAND'S ROYAL PRISONER

Queen Mary and her friends landed at Workington on the English coast at seven o'clock in the evening. The next day the Deputy Governor of Carlisle Castle and 100 soldiers arrived to escort the Queen to Carlisle. At Carlisle the Queen was watched by guards all the time. She had come to England looking for help but instead she had been made a prisoner.

Queen Mary had expected help from Queen Elizabeth but the English Queen refused to see her. She did not really want to help Queen Mary because she felt threatened by the Scottish Queen. Queen Elizabeth was well aware that some people thought that Queen Mary should be Queen of England instead of her. Rather than seeing Queen Mary straight away, Queen Elizabeth said she would see her when all the questions about Darnley's murder had been answered.

Queen Mary was given the chance to clear her name at a meeting in York in October 1568. The Earl of Moray was at the meeting too. He wanted to prove that both Queen Mary and Bothwell were involved in Darnley's murder. Moray had one important piece of evidence which he thought would show that this was true. He claimed he had a box which belonged to Bothwell. The box was supposed to contain letters from the Queen to Bothwell which told of Darnley's murder. These letters became known as the 'Casket Letters' and were thought to be forgeries. Queen Elizabeth sent a group of noblemen to listen to the evidence from both sides. The English noblemen were unable to reach a decision one way or the other. Queen Mary remained a prisoner of the English.

To pass the time while she was being kept a prisoner, Queen Mary did a lot of embroidery. You can see a piece of Queen Mary's embroidery in Holyrood Palace. The ideas for the embroidered pictures came from books of animals and plants. The pictures were copied on to canvas before being sewn.

The box which contained the 'Casket Letters' can be seen at Lennoxlove House, outside Haddington, now the home of the Duke of Hamilton.

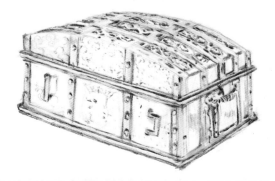

Answers on page 40

Hidden in this wordsearch are the names of 12 creatures which Queen Mary embroidered. Can you find them?

```
P A T O U C A N R B
H A Y F J A N E U D
E E L L G T G H N R
A L F L S I T M I E
S E R I T U X Q C I
A P E A V O Z N O N
N H T N R A A K R D
T A T S I V M E N E
C N U N O I L Y P E
G T E O V E R E R
```

QUEEN MARY'S TRIAL AND EXECUTION

For the next 19 years (1568 – 87), Queen Mary was moved from one prison to another. Mary Seton was allowed to join Queen Mary in England to help look after her. There were several plots to get Queen Mary out of prison. One of these plots involved making Queen Mary the Queen of England instead of Queen Elizabeth.

Queen Elizabeth was worried about the plots. She did not want to lose her throne and gave Sir Francis Walsingham the job of finding the people who were plotting against her. Sir Francis Walsingham particularly wanted to catch Queen Mary plotting against his own Queen.

After the last failed plot, Queen Mary was not allowed to write any letters. Writing letters had been Queen Mary's only way to keep in contact with the outside world. When she was approached by someone who agreed to carry letters secretly for her she was very pleased. What she did not know was that this person was working for Sir Francis Walsingham. Any letters Queen Mary wrote or received went to Sir Francis first and then on to where they were supposed to go. This was how the Babington Plot was discovered. A group of young English noblemen planned to free Queen Mary and make her Queen of England instead of Queen Elizabeth.

In my end is my beginning

Queen Mary's trial started on 15th October 1586 in Fotheringay Castle, Northamptonshire. She was charged with plotting to kill Queen Elizabeth. Queen Mary had to speak in her own defence because she was not allowed to have a lawyer. She was found guilty.

During her time in prison Queen Mary hoped that one day her son, King James VI of Scotland, would rescue her. But James had been brought up by his tutor to hate and fear his mother so he did not try to set her free. In July 1586 Queen Mary got some very bad news. Her son had signed a peace treaty with Queen Elizabeth and was going to receive money from her. This made Queen Mary very upset. She wrote a letter to Sir Anthony Babington agreeing to his plans. Sir Francis Walsingham had trapped Queen Mary.

Queen Mary's tomb at Westminster Abbey

James VI of Scotland

When Queen Elizabeth I of England died in 1603, King James VI of Scotland became King of England too. He felt sad and possibly guilty about the way Queen Mary had been treated.

He had Fotheringay Castle demolished and his mother's body moved to a marble tomb in Westminster Abbey.

Early in the morning on 8th February 1587, Queen Mary was executed in the Great Hall at Fotheringay Castle.

PLACES TO VISIT AND ANSWERS

Here is a list of places associated with Mary, Queen of Scots. They are either places where Mary, Queen of Scots stayed or places which have displays of interesting items relating to her.

- Linlithgow Palace
- Stirling Castle
- Dumbarton Castle
- Inchmahome Priory, Lake of Menteith
- Holyrood Palace, Edinburgh
- John Knox House, Edinburgh
- Falkland Palace, Fife
- Traquair House, Borders
- Mary, Queen of Scots House, Jedburgh, Borders
- Edinburgh Castle
- Craigmillar Castle, Edinburgh
- Lochleven Castle, Fife
- Dundrennan Abbey, Dumfries and Galloway
- Lennoxlove House, East Lothian
- Scottish National Portrait Gallery, Edinburgh - 'Dynasty' Exhibition

As the opening times of these places vary it would be a good idea to check opening time details with the local Tourist Information Office.

Pages 2 & 3
80 words - There may be more! (eg glisten, elongate, nail, long, saline, tone)

Pages 4 & 5
8 creatures - snail, swan, newt, duck, fish, otter, frog, beetle.

Pages 6 & 7
Diamond - clear;
emerald - green;
ruby - red;
sapphire - blue;
garnet - deep red;
peridot - green;
turquoise - clear/blue;
amethyst - purple.

Pages 8 & 9
pig, pallet, petticoat, plant, plate, periscope, parcel, pick, puddle, pansy, puppy, pie, priory.

Pages 10 & 11
7 small dogs.

Pages 12 & 13
'Long Live Queen Mary'.

Pages 14 & 15
'Mary, Mary Quite Contrary'.

Pages 18 & 19
TV aerial, venetian blinds, doorbell, roller skates, ice-cream, stereo headphones, drain, parking meter, training shoes.

Pages 22 & 23
Flavours: cloves, saffron, nutmeg, ginger, vinegar, olive oil.

Pages 28 & 29
'Who killed Lord Darnley?'

Pages 30 & 31
hat badge, moustache, sword, sleeve top detail, pendant.

Pages 34 & 35
Linlithgow, Stirling, Edinburgh, Falkland, Lochleven, Dumbarton.
Arquebus - gun
Pike - long spear.

Pages 36 & 37

The End

P	A	T	O	U	C	A	N	R	B
H	A	Y	F	J	A	N	E	U	D
E	E	L	L	Q	T	G	H	N	R
A	L	F	L	S	I	T	M	I	E
S	E	R	I	T	U	X	O	C	I
A	P	E	A	W	O	Z	N	O	N
N	H	T	N	R	A	A	K	R	D
T	A	T	S	I	V	M	E	N	E
C	N	U	N	O	I	L	Y	P	E
G	T	B	E	A	V	E	R	E	R